THE WIZARD OF ID
YIELD

by Brant Parker and Johnny Hart

FAWCETT GOLD MEDAL • NEW YORK

THE WIZARD OF ID/YIELD

Copyright © 1968, 1969 by Publishers Newspaper Syndicate

© 1974 CBS Publications, The Consumer
Publishing Division of CBS Inc.

Published by special arrangement with
Publishers-Hall Syndicate, Inc.

ISBN: 0-449-13653-1

Printed in the United States of America

19   18   17   16   15   14   13   12   11   10

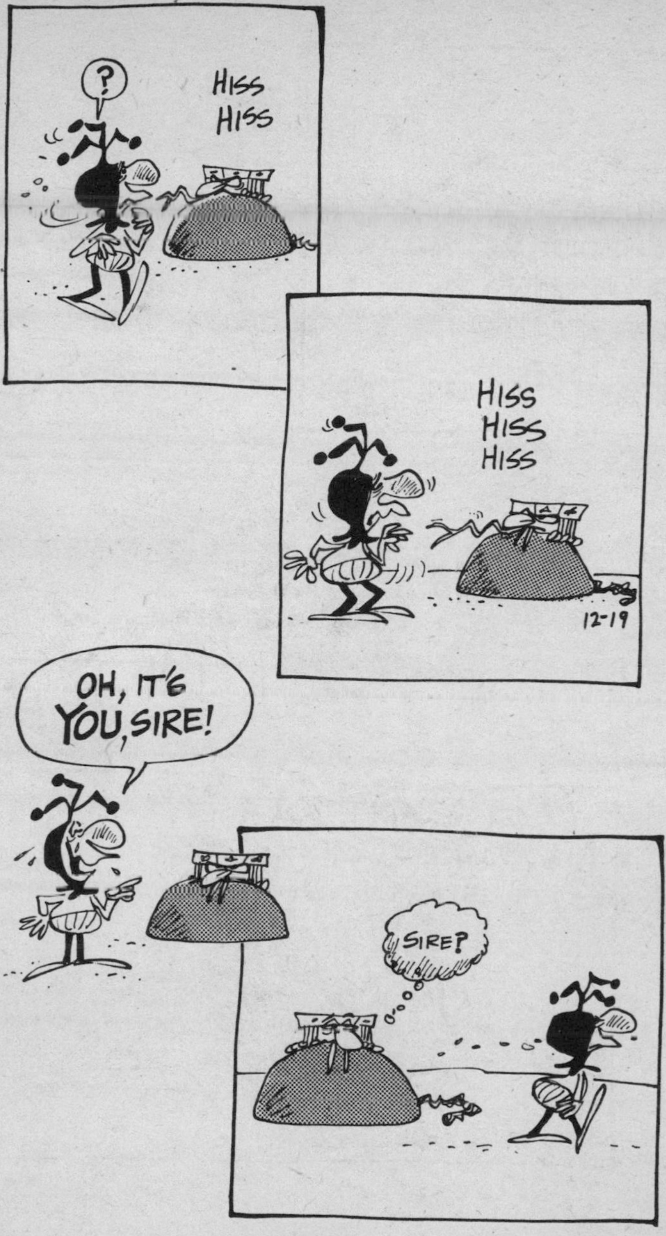
?
HISS
HISS
HISS
HISS
HISS
12-19
OH, IT'S YOU, SIRE!
SIRE?

GOOD NEWS, SIRE!...

SQUISH SQUISH

... THE ENEMY HAS RUN OUT OF STONES.

1-9

WHAT DO YOU **THINK?**

I LIKED THE BOOK BETTER.

1-14

BONG

WHAT'S WRONG WITH THE BELL?

BONG

IT'S IN THE REPAIR SHOP.

1-16

1-29

IT IS WRITTEN, THAT WHOEVER PULLS THE GREAT SWORD OUT OF THE STONE, SHALL SUCCEED ME TO THE THRONE.
4-30
SET IT UP, AND GIVE EVERYBODY A TRY.
RIGHT AWAY, SIRE.
HOW ABOUT, WHOEVER CAN STICK IT INTO THE STONE?

5-9

In the *Wizard of Id* Series

THE KING IS A FINK	1-3709-0	$1.25
THE PEASANTS ARE REVOLTING	1-3671-X	$1.25
REMEMBER THE GOLDEN RULE	1-3717-1	$1.25
THERE'S A FLY IN MY SWILL	1-3687-6	$1.25
THE WONDROUS WIZARD OF ID	1-3648-5	$1.25
THE WIZARD'S BACK	1-3654-X	$1.25
THE WIZARD OF ID—YIELD	1-3653-1	$1.25
THE WIZARD OF ID #8	1-3681-7	$1.25
LONG LIVE THE KING	1-3655-8	$1.25
WE'VE GOT TO STOP MEETING LIKE THIS	1-3633-7	$1.25
EVERY MAN IS INNOCENT UNTIL PROVEN BROKE	1-3650-7	$1.25
I'M OFF TO SEE THE WIZARD	1-3700-7	$1.25